CW01594089

Fill up All day Brunch Yeah!
I need a new Swimming cap & Beach Sandals
Burger & Fries and a Comic Yeah!
Self catering.. .. so I need... Washing up liquid Fresh Veg Salad Cream ----
WE ARE OFF

Vincent Duffy

DUFFY'S CHEAPER CHOICES

Alternatives to motorway service stations

Amadeus Publications

Amadeus Publications
Atlas House
Quarry Terrace
Horsforth
Leeds LS18 4EH

Tel: 0113 258 1289

Printed by The Amadeus Press Ltd
West 26 Business Park, Cleckheaton, BD19 4TQ

This book is sold subject to the condition that it shall not be lent, resold, hired out or otherwise circulated without the publisher's prior written consent. No part of this publication may be reproduced in any form without the prior written permission of the publisher.

ISBN 0 9532284 2 8

First published 1999.
This edition published 2000.

This book is dedicated to my wife, Denise.

FOREWORD

The opinions expressed herein are entirely my own even if, as I suspect, they are shared by the vast majority of the population. It is my belief that the motorway service stations enjoy a monopoly position which is completely undeserved.

Their food, drink and petrol are overpriced compared to the outlets in this book and there are times when they are overcrowded for an all too obvious reason: the unfortunate motorway driver is a captive customer, he does not know where else to go.

The purpose of this book is to provide the driver with cheaper alternatives close to motorway junctions which sell hot food, petrol and have toilet facilities.

The idea occurred in conversation. I had already written a book (see note at the end of this foreword) and my wife, Denise, and I were mulling over this and other topics. It was the night of 29th July 1998 and we were in the bar of the "White House" at Whitby, a favourite haunt. Denise suggested a list of pubs as being alternatives to these service stations on motorways. This book is the natural development of that discussion.

I put the thought to Tesco and Sainsbury's. They each immediately instructed their research departments to produce a suitable list which forms the nucleus of this book. As the reader can see, almost 80% of my "cheaper choices" are the large modern supermarkets which offer excellent value for money in terms of a cooked breakfast and the price of petrol when compared with motorway service stations.

Whilst I have concentrated on the popular choice, i.e. the all day breakfast, the menus are varied and the salads, lunches and desserts are appetising at the venues named in this book. Furthermore, the customer invariably has the opportunity for shopping on the move as it were, an invaluable asset on a family holiday.

By and large I have endeavoured to obtain outlets as close to the junction as possible. Discounting the four at Huntingdon, Gravesend, Queensferry and Plymouth which are included as extensions to motorways, the average distance is 0.85 mile. That arithmetic/achievement pleases me.

The service stations do not have a pure monopoly because there are alternatives. That is why I have written this book. I wish to provide these "cheaper choices", allow full rein to free market forces and let the public make their own decisions. The success of my work will reflect the extent to which I have performed that function. I hope you, the reader, share my sentiments.

V.P. Duffy

May 1999

"Duffy's 41": The best pub fish and chips in Yorkshire

Published 1998

FOREWORD TO THE NEW EDITION

On the 8th March 2000 I was asked to do an interview on my book for "You and Yours" which is on Radio Four at midday Monday to Friday. The interview was duly broadcasted the following Monday and the response was amazing. Immediately I was recalled to link up at various times from Radio Leeds to around 12 local stations throughout the country. This was followed by Radio Five "Drive" and even the British Forces overseas network.

All in all the demand surged ahead, I had run low on copies and put in hand this edition which has 3 additional outlets. I have received many letters from satisfied readers and print some of them in the book with their kind permission. It is of the utmost importance what the reader thinks and what he or she wants. I am more than happy to print their views. They provide ample justification for my idea to write such a book.

If you, the reader, have any suggestions, please write to me at the publisher's address or even telephone me at my office in Horsforth, Leeds. I hope the book is both useful and interesting.

V.P. Duffy
April 2000

Tesco
Jarman Way
Hemel Hempstead

M1/Junction 8

Tel: 01442 420400

Location:	At junction 8 take the A414 into Hemel Hempstead. Tesco is on the left at the fourth roundabout 1.9 miles from the junction.	
Hours:	Monday - Friday	8.00 a.m. - 8.00 p.m.
	Saturday	7.00 a.m. - 8.00 p.m.
	Sunday	10.00 a.m. - 4.00 p.m.
Description:	The New Magnificent 7 at £1.99 is available until noon. The all day brunch is £2.99.	
Petrol:	On site 24 hours, 7 days.	
Comments:	Almost equally accessible from junction 20 M25 via the A41 and turn right onto the A414.	

Tesco **_M1/Junction 11_**
Skinpot Road
Dunstable

Tel: 01582 687500

Location: At junction 11 take the A505 to Dunstable. The store is on the left at the first roundabout 0.7 mile from the junction.

Hours:

Monday	8.00 a.m. - 8.00 p.m.
Tuesday - Saturday	8.00 a.m. - 7.00 p.m.
Sunday	10.00 a.m. - 4.00 p.m.

Description: The New Magnificent 7 is available till noon and costs £1.99. The all day brunch is £2.99.

Petrol: On site 24 hours, 7 days.

Comments: Pat, in the restaurant, told me about the popularity of the breakfast with passing travellers and the local inhabitants. Incidentally, the restaurant area used to be a McDonald's. "Well, well, well", said I.

Truckstop *M1/Junction 18*
A5
Rugby

Tel: 01788 535115

Location: From junction 18 take the A428 towards Rugby. Take the A5 at the first roundabout and Truckstop is on the right hand side fronting the A5 and 2.5 miles from junction 18.

Hours: Open 24 hours a day apart from 2.00 p.m. on Saturday until 8.00 a.m. on Sunday.

Description: All day breakfast £3.99 includes sausages, bacon, egg, hash browns and beans.

Petrol: Available on site 24 hours.

Comments: Not just an HGV venue, this facility is spotless, has a shop and shower facilities on site, the restaurant is in the design of a Swedish log cabin and the cottage pie at £4.99 looked particularly appetizing. Totally appropriate for a family stop off.

The Wheatsheaf *M1/Junction 18*
15 Main Road
Crick

Tel: 01788 822284

Location:	Take the A428 east of junction 18, the pub is on the left 0.9 mile from junction 18.	
Hours:	Monday - Saturday	Noon - 2.30 p.m. and 6.00 p.m. - 9.30 p.m.
	Sunday	Noon - 10.30 p.m.
Landlords:	Susan and Christopher Lee.	
Description:	Extensive menu, please consult the blackboard too. The pies are home made.	
Petrol:	Available 0.75 mile past the pub towards Northampton on the left hand side,	
	Monday - Friday	7.00 a.m. - 6.30 p.m.
	Saturday	7.00 a.m. - 5.00 p.m.
	Sunday	Closed.
Comments:	A pleasant dark stone pub in a rustic setting backing onto the church, the pub was first referred to in 1770 and plays host to a ghost who had a penchant for playing skittles. There's something about a village pub that dissipates the tension generated by long hours on the motorway.	

Asda *M1/Junction 21*
Narborough Road South
Leicester

Tel: 0116 289 8174

Location: Take the dual carriageway east of junction 21 towards Leicester. Asda fronts the main road 0.7 mile from this junction.

Hours: Monday 8.00 a.m. until Saturday 10.00 p.m. open 24 hours per day,
Sunday 10.00 a.m. until 4.00 p.m.

Description: The set breakfast comprising 10 items costs £2.79 and is available until 11.30 a.m. It includes 2 sausages, 2 bacon rashers, 2 hash browns, egg, beans, tomato, mushrooms plus any hot drink. After 11.30 a.m. the all day brunch comes into play at the same price where chips replace the hash browns, tomato and mushrooms. There is also a 6 of the best breakfast at £1.79.

Petrol: Monday 8.00 a.m. until Saturday 10.00 p.m. open 24 hours.
Sunday 10.00 a.m. until 4.00 p.m.

Comments: Forms part of the Fosse Park complex including a large out of town Marks and Spencer. Very convenient for the M1.

Sainsbury's *Fosse Park* *Leicester*

M1/Junction 21

Tel: 0116 263 1153

Location: At junction 21 take the road to Leicester. Turn right at the first roundabout and the store is on the right. Turn right at the lights for access. The supermarket is 0.8 mile from the junction.

Hours:

Monday - Wednesday	8.00 a.m. - 7.30 p.m.
Thursday	8.00 a.m. - 8.30 p.m.
Friday	8.00 a.m. - 9.30 p.m.
Saturday	7.30 a.m. - 7.30 p.m.
Sunday	9.00 a.m. - 3.30 p.m.

Description: The breakfast at £1.95 is served until noon. The all day brunch is £3.10 and an all day breakfast also at £3.10 comprises 2 sausages, bacon, fried egg, hash browns, mushrooms, beans and fried bread.

Petrol: On site 24 hours, 7 days.

Comments: Forms part of the prestigious Fosse Park complex. The staff proudly informed me it is popular with eminent members of Leicester City F.C. Curiously only today as I write this, I read in the property press that the developers are trying to rename the Park as Blaby town centre. Oh dear!

SAINSBURY'S ALL DAY BRUNCH
YUM YUM
£3-10

Field Head Hotel ***M1/Junction 22***
Markfield Lane
Leicester

Tel: 01530 245454

Location: At junction 22 take the A50 into Leicester. After 1 mile the hotel is on the other side of the roundabout.

Landlord: Andrew Garforth.

Hours: Food is usually served at the following times.

Monday - Saturday	Noon - 2.00 p.m.
	7.00 p.m. - 9.30 p.m.
Sunday	Noon - 9.30 p.m.

However, I am told by Andrew the landlord that if you wish to ring say 24 hours in advance, the management will be happy to prepare cooked food beyond the range of sandwiches outside of these hours.

Description: Too various to list here. I had the large Yorkshire Pudding filled with sausages and onion gravy at £4.00. Marvellous!

Petrol: There is a petrol station at junction 22 immediately on the west side open 24 hours, 7 days.

Comments: A lovely local stone building dating back to 1672 which was a farmhouse. At the risk of being repetitive a pub does dissipate motorway tension. There are tales that in the original farmhouse part of the building is seen a stressful lady ghost carrying a baby twixt house and barn. My gratitude to my good friend Michael O'Donnell for mentioning this venue.

The Broxtowe Inn ***M1/Junction 26***
Nottingham Road
Nuthall
Nottingham

Tel: 0115 927 8210

Location: Take the A610 east of junction 26 towards Nottingham. The pub is on the right 0.7 mile from this junction.

Hours:

Monday - Saturday	Noon - 9.30 p.m.
Sunday	Noon - 8.30 p.m.

Landlady: Vanessa Scrimshaw.

Description: Good all round menu. My favourite was Theakston sausage and mash at £4.25.

Petrol: Immediately adjacent open 24 hours per day, 7 days a week.

Comments: Had a fascinating conversation with Alfred Cresswell, aged 74, who has been a regular here for 60 years. The pub now backs onto the new bypass (A610) and faces the quiet old road into the city. Situated in the depths of a mining area, (Babbington pit now closed) those immediately off the shift had to sit in the porch whilst the regulars fetched their pint from the bar. It was then, said Alfred, 4 pence a pint (just over 1.5 new pence).

McArthur Glen *M1/Junction 28*
Designer Outlet Village

Tel: 01773 545000

Location:	0.7 mile east of junction 28, leave the first slip road and the development is visible over to the right.
Hours:	Monday - Friday 9.00 a.m. - 6.00 p.m. Thursday Opens until 8.00 p.m. Saturday 8.00 a.m. - 6.00 p.m. Sunday 10.00 a.m. - 5.00 p.m.
Description:	The "Foodcourt" caters for all tastes with an English restaurant doing a full breakfast at £3.25 plus Arkwrights fish and chips, Singapore Sam's chinese food and Spud U Like.
Petrol:	Available 24 hours, 7 days 0.5 mile further down the A38 on the left hand side.
Comments:	A shopping village selling designer clothes, household goods, footwear and homewear. Expensive stock at reduced prices that still looked expensive to me.

Lets try plan B...

The Sportsman *M1/Junction 35*
Upper Wortley Road
Rotherham

Tel: 0114 257 2011

Location: Fronts A629 0.9 mile from junction 35 in the direction of Rotherham.

Hours:

Monday - Saturday	11.30 a.m. - 2.30 p.m. and 5.00 a.m. - 9.00 p.m.
Sunday	Noon - 6.00 p.m.

Landlord: Tony Griffiths

Description: All day breakfast £3.45.

Petrol: Adjacent Esso station open 24 hours, 7 days.

Comments: The original structure of the pub was part of Kirkstead Abbey and ghostly sightings have taken place in several parts of the building including, apparently, a whistling ghost. Formerly the gaming rooms of the Earl of Wentworth. Excellent fare at this venue.

The Old Malt Shovel *M1/Junction 40*
Dewsbury Road
Wakefield

Tel: 01924 201561

Location: On A638 0.3 mile from junction 40.

Hours: Monday - Saturday 8.00 a.m. - 3.00 p.m.

Landlord: Steve Quirke.

Description: Bacon, egg, sausages, black pudding, fried bread, beans or tomatoes, tea or coffee: £2.50

Petrol: Esso station between the public house and motorway open 24 hours.

Comments: Steve asked me to mention the truckers' lunch from noon till 3.00 p.m. comprising a roast dinner at £2.50 being beef, lamb or pork.

Morrisons *M1/Junction 40*
Dewsbury Road
Wakefield

Tel: 01924 201655

Location: 1.2 miles from junction 40. Take the A638 towards Wakefield, the supermarket is on the left.

Hours:

Monday, Tuesday, Wednesday	8.30 a.m. - 7.00 p.m.
Thursday, Friday	8.30 a.m. - 8.00 p.m.
Saturday	8.00 a.m. - 6.00 p.m.
Sunday	10.00 a.m. - 4.00 p.m.

Description: Morrisons famous big breakfast, bacon, sausage, egg, mushrooms, beans, fried bread, hash brown £2.89.

Petrol: On site

Monday - Saturday	7.00 a.m. - 10.00 p.m.
Sunday	7.30 a.m. - 7.00 p.m.

Comments: Excellent value, good all round menu.

Sainsbury's Colton Retail Park Leeds — *M1/Junction 46*

Tel: 0113 232 8151

Location:	At junction 46 take the A6120 to Leeds. The store is on the left hand side 0.25 mile from the junction.	
Hours:	Monday - Wednesday	8.30 a.m. - 6.30 p.m.
	Thursday and Friday	8.30 a.m. - 7.30 p.m.
	Saturday	8.30 a.m. - 6.30 p.m.
	Sunday	11.00 a.m. - 5.00 p.m.
Description:	Breakfast followed by the brunch at 11.30 a.m. is £3.10. There is a breakfast at £1.95 which is smaller and a double breakfast £3.60.	
Petrol:	On site	
	Monday - Saturday	6.00 a.m. - 10.30 p.m.
	Sunday	7.00 a.m. - 9.00 p.m.
Comments:	Forms part of the M1 extension linking into the A1 for northbound traffic.	

The Bushe Partnership
29 Maddox Street, Mayfair, London W1R 9LD
Tel: (44) 0171 491 4791 Fax: (44) 0171 491 8550
Mobile: (44) 07979 852 240

V Duffy Esq
Duffy & Co
Atlas House
Quarry Terrace
Horsforth
Leeds LS 18 4EH

Tuesday, 12th October 1999

Dear Vince

Thank you very much for the book!

It has proved very useful over the last two months, particularly where my family have been involved. Our summer holiday in Scotland and a weekend in Cornwall were certainly enhanced by our quality breakfast stops, having set out before 5.30 am on each occasion!

I have to say it was received with a certain amount of scepticism until the first time we stopped. I think they thought we'd be spending travel time hunting for these places but soon discovered that the quality, ease and fun of Sainsbury's or Tesco's outweighed the mad scramble and mess of the motorway stops. As I have to feed 5 people at a time, I also noticed the difference!

I have sent my second copy to the family that we were traveling with and will call you as and when I need further copies.

I will let you know when I am next heading for Leeds, please give me a call if you are coming to London.

Kind regards

David Bushe

Sainsbury's *M3/Junction 4*
Blackwater Valley Road
Camberley

Tel: 01276 676829

Location: At junction 4 take the A331 north to Camberley. The store is on the right hand side 0.2 mile from the junction.

Hours:

Monday - Wednesday	8.00 a.m. - 7.00 p.m.
Thursday and Friday	8.00 a.m. - 7.30 p.m.
Saturday	7.30 a.m. - 7.00 p.m.
Sunday	9.30 a.m. - 4.00 p.m.

Description: The brunch at £3.10 is available all day. The breakfast is at £1.95 until 11.30 a.m.

Petrol: On site 24 hours, 7 days.

Comments: This is a prestige store currently being extended and refurbished. Very convenient for the motorway and what is more I was informed that Matthew Corbet had visited without, unfortunately, Sooty, who was otherwise engaged.

Sainsbury's *M4/Junction 7*
Lake End Road
Taplow

Tel: 01628 661529

Location: Leave junction 7 and take the slip road to the A4. Turn left on the A4 and the store is 0.5 mile from this junction on the left hand side.

Hours:

Monday - Thursday	8.30 a.m. - 8.30 p.m.
Friday	8.30 a.m. - 10.00 p.m.
Saturday	8.00 a.m. - 7.30 p.m.
Sunday	9.30 a.m. - 4.30 p.m.

Description: All day brunch is £3.10. The single breakfast is £1.95 and the double breakfast is £3.60. The single comprises sausage, bacon, egg, beans, hash brown, tomato and toast. The double is very popular with the locals.

Petrol: Not on site, however it is available 24 hours a day if at the A4 junction with the slip road turn right and the facility is 0.5 mile on the right.

Comments: Thank you Richard Morris, the restaurant manager, for the cup of tea and hospitality.

Savacentre *M4/Junction 12*

Bath Road
Calcot
Reading

Tel: 0118 938 2200

Location: At junction 12 take the A4 into Reading. The store is on the left hand side at the second roundabout around 0.2 mile from the junction.

Hours:

Monday - Wednesday	8.00 a.m. - 7.00 p.m.
Thursday	8.00 a.m. - 8.00 p.m.
Friday	8.00 a.m. - 9.00 p.m.
Saturday	8.00 a.m. - 7.00 p.m.
Sunday	9.00 a.m. - 4.00 p.m.

Description: All day brunch £2.35. Any 6 item breakfast £2.95. Any 9 item breakfast £3.45.

Petrol: On site

Monday	6.00 a.m. - 11.00 p.m.
Tuesday	6.00 a.m. - midnight
Wednesday & Thursday	5.00 a.m. - midnight
Friday	5.00 a.m. - 10.30 p.m.
Saturday and Sunday	6.00 a.m. - 10.30 p.m.

Comments: Something of a flagship store following refurbishment and very convenient from the M4.

Asda *M4/Junction 16*
West Swindon District Centre
Tewkesbury Way
Swindon

Tel: 01793 872781

Location:	At junction 16 take the A3102 to Swindon. Turn left at the first roundabout, the District Centre is sign posted, and Asda is at the fourth roundabout thereafter 1.9 miles from the junction.	
Hours:	Monday - Friday	8.30 a.m. - 10.00 p.m.
	Saturday	8.30 a.m. - 8.00 p.m.
	Sunday	10.00 a.m. - 4.00 p.m.
Description:	Asda big breakfast £2.79 comprises 2 sausages, 2 bacon rashers, fried egg, beans, hash browns, mushrooms, tomato and tea or coffee. This is available until 11.30 a.m. and thereafter replaced by the Asda big brunch at the same price where chips substitute for the hash browns.	
Petrol:	On site Monday - Saturday	7.00 a.m. -10.15 p.m.
	Sunday	9.00 a.m. - 6.00 p.m.
Comments:	Part of a shopping mall, I was informed that Steve McMahon, the Manager of Swindon Town is a regular shopper here as well as Clive Mantle, a "Casualty" star who, coincidentally, was appearing that night in "The Price" by Arthur Miller at the Bristol Old Vic. Ideal for West Country traffic from London and the south-east.	

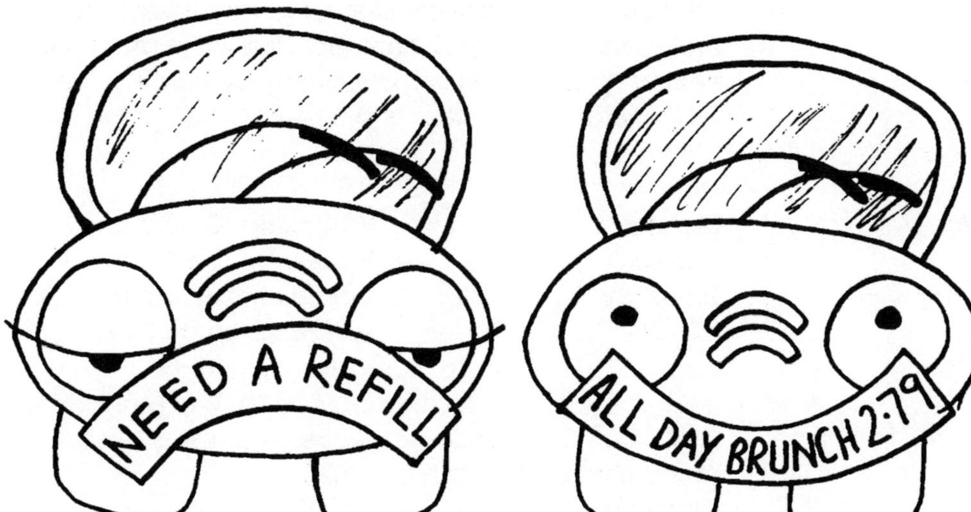
NEED A REFILL
ALL DAY BRUNCH 2.79

Savacentre   *M5/Junction 2*

Freeth Street
Oldbury
Birmingham

Tel: 0121 665 2900

Location: Leave junction 2 and go to the roundabout. Take the right turn A4034 sign posted Oldbury and the store is facing you when you approach the next roundabout behind that temple of epicurean delectation called McDonald's. The store is 0.7 mile from junction 2.

Hours:

Monday - Thursday	8.00 a.m. - 6.30 p.m.
Friday	8.00 a.m. - 7.30 p.m.
Saturday	7.00 a.m. - 6.30 p.m.
Sunday	9.30 a.m. - 4.00 p.m.

Description:

Any 6 item breakfast	£2.95
Any 9 item breakfast	£3.45
All day brunch	£2.35

Petrol:

On site Monday - Saturday	6.00 a.m. - 10.00 p.m.
Sunday	8.00 a.m. - 6.30 p.m.

Comments: Don't be put off by the busy conurbation. It is actually very easy to find and offers excellent fare.

The Oak Apple Inn | *M5/Junction 7*

Spetchley Road
Worcester

Tel: 01905 355121

Location: At junction 7 take the A44 sign posted "Worcester (City Centre)". The pub is on the right at the third roundabout 1.1 miles from the junction.

Hours:

Monday - Thursday	Noon - 9.00 p.m.
Friday - Sunday	Noon - 10.00 p.m.

Landlady: Tina Woodall.

Description: Too numerous to cite all but there is a very good home made Lasagne at £4.80. Andy Mason, the chef, is proud of the Sunday roast of beef, lamb or pork whereby a two course lunch including home made soup is available at £5.95.

Petrol: Immediately next door

Monday - Friday	7.00 a.m. - 10.00 p.m.
Saturday	7.00 a.m. - 9.00 p.m.
Sunday	8.00 a.m. - 9.00 p.m.

Comments: A modern pub very popular with the local population which is always a good sign.

Safeway *M5/Junction 9*
Ashchurch Road
Tewkesbury

Tel: 01684 273261

Location:	From junction 9 take the A438 into Tewkesbury. The store is on the right 0.9 mile from the junction.

Hours:

Monday - Thursday	8.00 a.m. - 7.30 p.m.
Friday	8.00 a.m. - 8.30 p.m.
Saturday	8.00 a.m. - 7.30 p.m.
Sunday	10.00 a.m. - 3.30 p.m.

Description: All day big breakfast at £1.99 comprises sausage, bacon, egg, hash brown, beans, tomato and toast. The big brunch commences at 11.30 a.m., costs £3.09 and comprises 2 sausages, 2 eggs, 2 bacon rashers, tomatoes or beans, chips, bread and butter.

Petrol:

On site Monday - Thursday	7.00 a.m. - 9.00 p.m.
Friday	7.00 a.m. - 10.00 p.m.
Saturday	7.00 a.m. - 9.00 p.m.
Sunday	9.00 a.m. - 5.00 p.m.

Comments: Yvonne in the restaurant proudly said that they will do take-aways of such as fish and chips and jacket potatoes and that coach parties can be catered for at 24 hours notice. Sharon Davies, the former Olympic swimmer, is a regular here.

Safeway *M5/Junction 21*
Locking Gate
Weston-Super-Mare

Tel: 01934 516577

Location: At junction 21 take the road to Weston-Super-Mare. Safeway is at the first roundabout 0.8 mile from the junction.

Hours:

Monday - Wednesday	8.00 a.m. - 9.00 p.m.
Thursday and Friday	8.00 a.m. - 10.00 p.m.
Saturday	8.00 a.m. - 9.00 p.m.
Sunday	10.00 a.m. - 4.00 p.m.

Description: The big breakfast till 11.30 a.m. at £1.99 comprises sausage, hash brown, bacon, fried egg, tomato, beans, toast, butter and marmalade. After 11.30 a.m. the brunch takes over at £3.09 comprising 2 sausages, 2 eggs, 2 bacon rashers, beans or tomatoes, chips, bread and butter.

Petrol:

On site Monday - Wednesday	6.00 a.m. - 10.00 p.m.
Thursday and Friday	6.00 a.m. - 10.30 p.m.
Saturday	6.00 a.m. - 10.00 p.m.
Sunday	8.00 a.m. - 10.00 p.m.

Comments: The restaurant, Dee proudly told me, has won a healthy eating award from Somerset County Council for the range and quality of its fare.

Tesco *M5/Junction 22*
Ben Travers Way
Burnham-on-Sea

Tel: 01278 463400

Location: At junction 22 go the roundabout immediately on the west side. Take the B3140 and the supermarket is at the first roundabout 1.5 miles from the junction.

Hours:

Monday - Friday	8.00 a.m. - 7.45 p.m.
Saturday	8.00 a.m. - 6.45 p.m.
Sunday	10.00 a.m. - 4.00 p.m.

Description: There is a New Magnificent 7 at £1.99 comprising bacon, sausage, egg, beans, tomato, hash browns, toast and butter.
The all day big brunch is £2.99.

Petrol: Not on site but it is available 24 hours, 7 days by continuing into Burnham 0.5 mile from the Tesco and the station is on the left hand side.

Comments: Motorway traffic and holiday makers in the locality as well as Wookey Hole and Cheddar Gorge fanatics make this a very popular summer venue.

Sainsbury's Heron Gate Taunton — *M5/Junction 25*

Tel: 01823 443163

Location: The store is immediately adjacent to and clearly visible from junction 25. Take the A358 on the west side of the motorway to Taunton and turn first right into the development.

Hours:

Monday - Thursday	8.00 a.m. - 7.00 p.m.
Friday	8.00 a.m. - 10.00 p.m.
Saturday	7.00 a.m. - 7.00 p.m.
Sunday	9.30 a.m. - 3.30 p.m.

Description: Apart from the usual all day brunch at £3.10, there is a double breakfast at £3.60 comprising 2 sausages, 2 bacon rashers, 2 fried eggs, beans or tomatoes, hash browns and toast.

Petrol: On site, 7 days 6.00 a.m. - midnight.

Comments: A brilliant location for Devon and Cornwall bound traffic. Charles Dance, Kate O'Mara, Andrew Caddick and Fern Britton of Ready Steady Cook have all frequented this store, none visible during my tour.

Tesco
Exeter Vale
Russell Way
Exeter

M5/Junction 30

Tel: 01392 607400

Location: At junction 30 take the A379 to Exeter. Follow the signs to the Tesco which take you left off this road, over it and to the other side being 1.2 miles from the junction and half that distance on returning to junction 30.

Hours:

Monday	8.00 a.m. - 8.00 p.m.
Tuesday - Thursday	7.00 a.m. - 8.00 p.m.
Friday	7.00 a.m. - 10.00 p.m.
Saturday	7.00 a.m. - 8.00 p.m.
Sunday	9.30 a.m. - 4.00 p.m.

Description: The all day brunch on Wednesday, 23rd March kept me going for a few hours.

Petrol: On site 24 hours, 7 days.

Comments: Michelle informed me that Cliff Richard, Nightshade of the Gladiators and James Hewitt have all frequented this store, not, I hasten to add, together.

HALIFAX

Our Ref: 0899PW/GEW

7th September 1999

Halifax plc
Group Treasury
33 Old Broad Street
London
EC2N 1HZ

Direct Line 0171 574 8158
Fax No 0171 574 8219

V. Duffy Esq.
c/o Amadeus Publications
Atlas House
Quarry Terrace
Horsforth
Leeds
LS18 4EH

Dear Mr Duffy

I bought a copy of Duffy's Cheaper Choices following the mention in "Property Week" and I have to tell you it is brilliant.

Taking my family (of seven) to Northumberland we saved twice the cost on the first (really excellent) breakfast alone, by a visit to Safeway at Newcastle Under Lyme – and was able to read the papers in an hour's peace by parking the children in the creche.

May you run to many editions – and for the next can I recommend Safeway at Berwick on Tweed, on the A1 roundabout north of the town – another excellent breakfast, and a MacDonalds next door.,

With regards,

Yours sincerely

P.A.B. Wilson
Head of Commercial Property Finance
Group Treasury

Sainsbury's *A38*
Plymouth Road
Plymouth

Tel: 01752 222748

Location: Lies at the junction of the A38 which is an extension of the M5 and A374 and backs onto the River Plym. Immensely conspicuous by virtue of its 11 Armada style sails which form part of the roof design.

Hours:

Monday - Thursday	8.00 a.m. - 8.00 p.m.
Friday	8.00 a.m. - 9.00 p.m.
Saturday	7.30 a.m. - 8.00 p.m.
Sunday	9.30 a.m. - 3.30 p.m.

Description: The all day brunch is £3.10 and comprises 2 sausages, 2 bacon rashers, fried or scrambled egg, chips, beans or tomato plus tea or coffee.

Petrol: On site 24 hours, 7 days.

Comments: Serendipity led me to this one. Brian, my brother, had suggested a trip to Plymouth to see a production of "Hamlet". On leaving Exeter to go to the hotel in Plymouth we drove past this store which was too good to miss. Despite not being on a motorway it was pleasing to secure another venue which pushes further in the West Country.

"A man may fish with the worm that hath eat of a king, and eat of the fish that hath fed of that worm".

Hamlet Act IV Scene III

Asda *M6/Junction 2*
Brade Drive
Coventry

Tel: 01203 613426

Location: Take the road due south of junction 2 to Coventry. Asda is on the left just past Toys R Us and 0.5 mile from junction 2. The store is equally accessible to the M69 which runs from junction 21 M1 to junction 2 M6.

Hours:

Monday - Wednesday	8.30 a.m. - 8.00 p.m.
Thursday and Friday	8.30 a.m. - 9.00 p.m.
Saturday	8.00 a.m. - 8.00 p.m.
Sunday	9.30 a.m. - 3.00 p.m.

Description: The set breakfast comprises 10 items until 11.30 a.m. Thereafter, the brunch is available, both at £2.79. There is some variety of selection over the breakfast items according to taste.

Petrol:

On site Monday - Saturday	5.00 a.m. - midnight
Sunday	6.00 a.m. - 10.00 p.m.

Comments: I was told by staff that the breakfast changes to the brunch because during the busy lunchtime people can take too long making up their minds. I can't work out if this is expedience or a tribute to market demand.

Sainsbury's *Voyager Drive* *Cannock* — *M6/Junction 11*

Tel: 01543 573757

Location: At junction 11 take the A460 into Cannock. Turn right onto the A5 and after 1 mile turn left, immediately after the railway bridge, into the Orbital Centre where Sainsbury's is on the right some 3 miles from the junction.

Hours:

Monday - Wednesday	9.30 a.m. - 6.30 p.m.
Thursday	8.30 a.m. - 7.00 p.m.
Friday	8.30 a.m. - 8.00 p.m.
Saturday	7.30 a.m. - 7.00 p.m.
Sunday	9.30 a.m. - 3.00 p.m.

Description: Breakfast at £1.95 lasts till 11.30 a.m. thereafter the brunch at £3.10 takes over. There is also a double breakfast at £3.60 until 11.30 a.m. comprising 2 fried eggs, 2 sausages, 2 bacon rashers, 2 hash browns, toast, beans or tomato.

Petrol:

Adjacent Monday - Friday	7.45 a.m. - 10.15 p.m.
Saturday	7.30 a.m. - 10.30 p.m.
Sunday	9.30 a.m. - 4.30 p.m.

Comments: Northbound traffic go straight up the A5 to junction 12.

Safeway — *M6/Junction 15*

Goose Street
Newcastle-Under-Lyme

Tel: 01782 710968

Location: At the roundabout adjacent to junction 15 take the A519 into Newcastle-Under-Lyme. The supermarket lies next to this road close to the town centre and 2.4 miles from the junction.

Hours:

Monday - Friday	8.00 a.m. - 10.00 p.m.
Saturday	7.30 a.m. - 8.00 p.m.
Sunday	10.00 a.m. - 4.00 p.m.

Description: Breakfast at £1.99 comprises fried egg, beans, tomato, 2 hash browns, bacon, sausage, toast and butter.

The brunch at £2.99 - 2 fried eggs, 2 bacon rashers, 2 sausages, beans, tomatoes, chips, bread and butter. The breakfast is served till 11.30 a.m. after which the brunch takes over.

Petrol: On site 24 hours, 7 days.

Comments: First class value. I had, on my visit, the breakfast at around 9.30 a.m. which kept me going till an evening meal at 7.00 p.m.

Sainsbury's *M6/Junction 29*

Cuerden Way
Bamber Bridge
Preston

Tel: 01772 627762

Location:

Leave junction 29 and take the M65 west towards Preston. At the roundabout take the right hand road (A6) and the store is 100 yards from this roundabout on the left hand side some 1.3 miles from junction 29.

Hours:

Monday - Thursday	8.30 a.m. - 6.00 p.m.
Friday	8.30 a.m. - 7.00 p.m.
Saturday	8.00 a.m. - 5.00 p.m.
Sunday	9.30 a.m. - 3.30 p.m.

Description:

The brunch is £3.10 and comprises 2 sausages, 2 bacon rashers, fried or scrambled egg, chips, beans or tomato.

Petrol:

Available on site

Monday - Saturday	6.00 a.m. - 10.00 p.m.
Sunday	7.00 a.m. - 10.00 p.m.

Comments:

This outlet links equally into the M61 (junction 9) via the aforementioned M65. The "5 after 5" (see Maidstone) is very popular.

HUNGRY
BIG BRUNCH 2·99

RUMBLE
RUMBLE
BIG BREAKFAST

The Plough Inn   *M6/Junction 33*

Main Road
Galgate
Lancaster

Tel: 01524 751337

Location: 0.6 mile west of junction 33. Take the road to the roundabout, turn right, the pub is on the left.

Hours:

Monday	11.30 a.m. - 2.30 p.m.
Wednesday - Saturday	11.30 a.m. - 2.30 p.m. and 6.30 p.m. - 8.30 p.m.
Sunday	Noon - 8.00 p.m.

Landlord: Mr Andrew Chapman.

Description: Whole spectrum of food from steaks at £5.50 to half roast chicken at £4.95

Comments: A pub since 1756, the year of Mozart's birth, this hostelry has a good deal of olde worlde charm. It backs onto Lancaster Canal and there is a pleasant marina adjacent. Worth a stop to escape the motorway hassle.

Truckhaven Limited *M6/Junction 35*

Scotland Road
Warton
Carnforth

Tel: 01524 736699

Location:	Take A601 (M) west of junction 35. Truckhaven is 0.9 mile from this junction on the left hand side.	
Hours:	Monday - Friday	5.30 a.m. - 10.30 p.m.
	Saturday	Closed
	Sunday	2.00 p.m. - 9.00 p.m.
Description:	All day breakfast comprises bacon, sausage, beans, egg, toast, tea or coffee £3.90.	
Petrol:	24 hours on site.	
Comments:	Comprehensive menu the breakfast apart. Massive car park, shop on site. Ideal stop off for Yorkshire Dales and Lake District traffic from the west side of the country.	

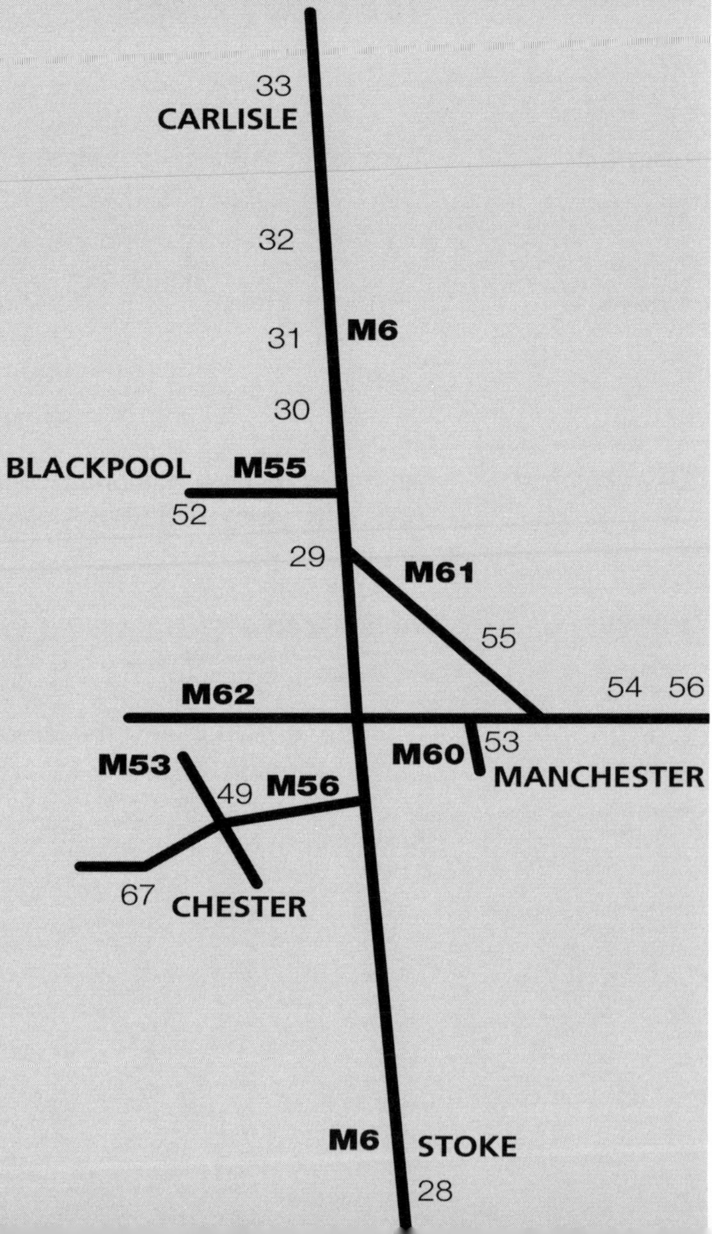
33
CARLISLE
32
31
M6
30
BLACKPOOL
M55
52
29
M61
55
54
56
M62
M60
53
MANCHESTER
M53
49
M56
67
CHESTER
M6
STOKE
28

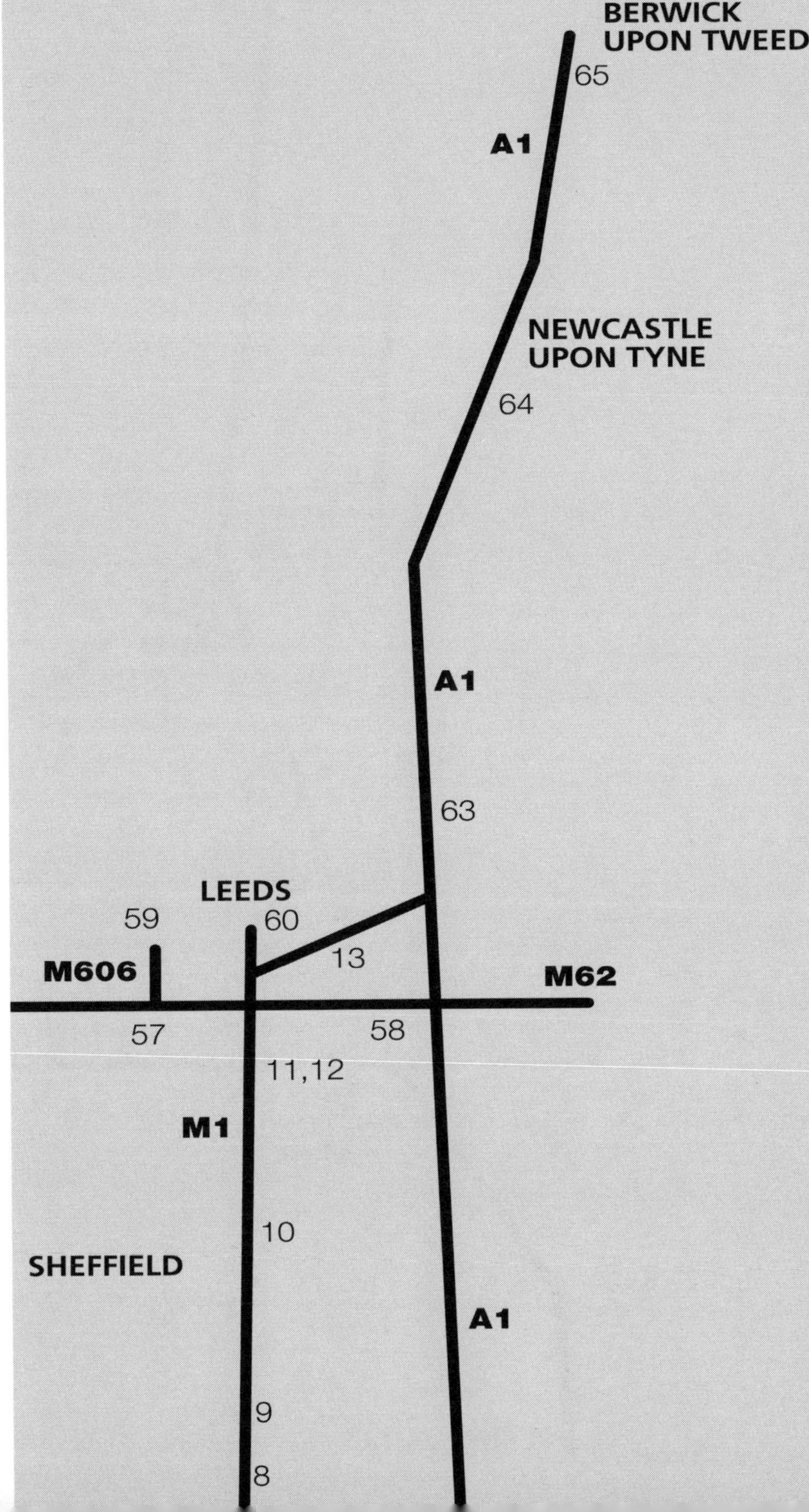
BERWICK
UPON TWEED
65
A1
NEWCASTLE
UPON TYNE
64
A1
63
LEEDS
59
60
13
M606
M62
57
58
11,12
M1
10
SHEFFIELD
A1
9
8

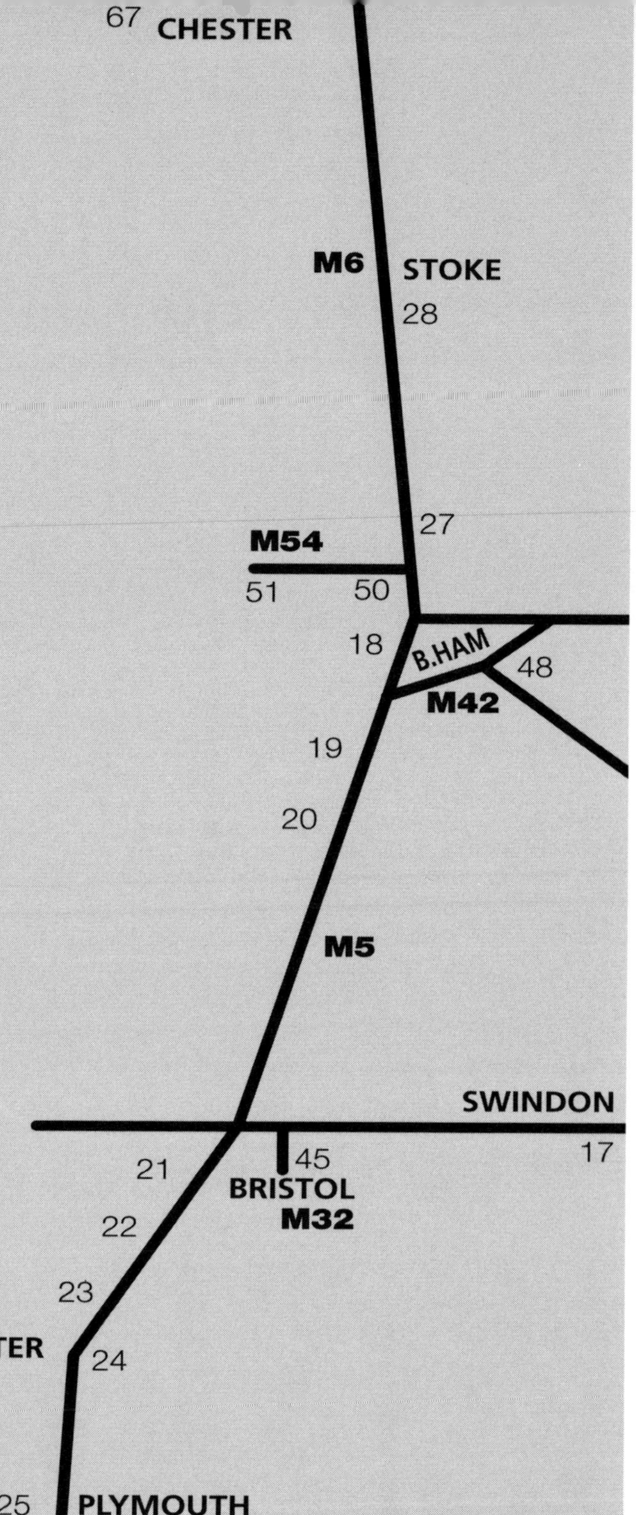
67 CHESTER
M6
STOKE
28
27
M54
51
50
18
B.HAM
48
M42
19
20
M5
SWINDON
17
21
45
BRISTOL
M32
22
23
EXETER
24
25
PLYMOUTH

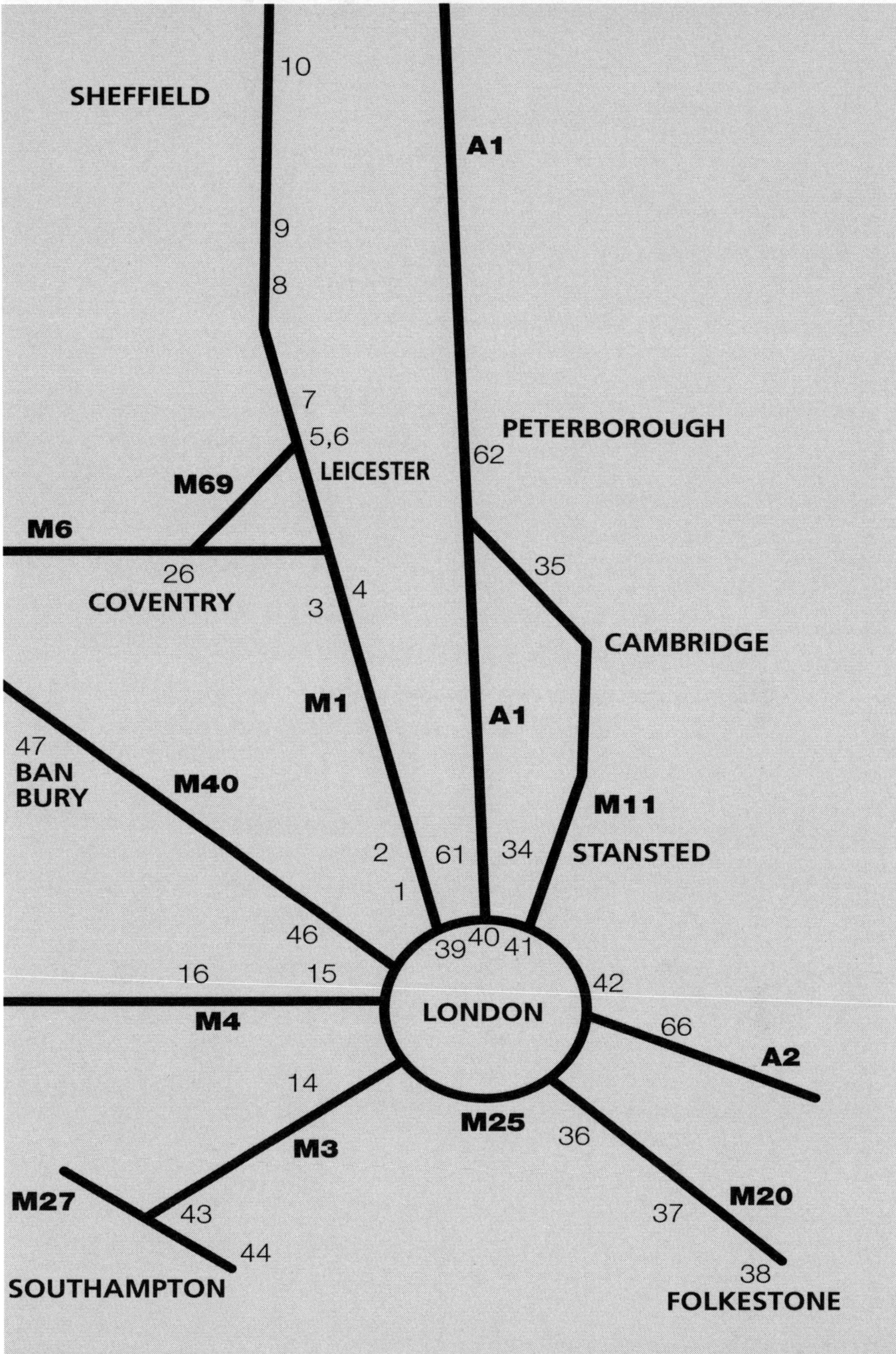

SHEFFIELD
10
A1
9
8
7
5,6
LEICESTER
PETERBOROUGH
62
M69
M6
26
COVENTRY
3
4
35
CAMBRIDGE
M1
A1
47
BAN
BURY
M40
M11
2
61
34
STANSTED
1
46
39
40
41
16
15
42
LONDON
M4
66
A2
14
M25
M3
36
M27
43
M20
37
44
38
SOUTHAMPTON
FOLKESTONE

Safeway *M6/Junction 40*
Brunswick Road
Penrith

Tel: 01768 867631

Location:	At junction 40 take the first exit on the east side showing "Penrith A592". The supermarket is at the second roundabout 0.75 mile from the junction.	
Hours:	Monday - Saturday Sunday	8.00 a.m. - 8.00 p.m. 10.00 a.m. - 4.00 p.m.
Description:	The all day breakfast at £1.99 comprises bacon, egg, beans, tomato, sausage, hash browns and toast, very adequate. There is also a brunch after 11.30 a.m. at £3.09.	
Petrol:	Monday - Saturday Sunday	7.00 a.m. - 10.00 p.m. 8.00 a.m. - 8.00 p.m.
Comments:	Apparently Chris Bonnington used to shop here. This store is one of three additions to my first book and the visit took place on the same day as my pleasant experience mentioned on page 33.	

Tesco
Warwick Road
Carlisle

M6/Junction 43

Tel: 01228 600400

Location:	Tesco is 500 yards from this junction clearly visible on the right hand side.
Hours:	Monday - Saturday 8.00 a.m. - 8.00 p.m. Sunday 10.00 a.m. - 4.00 p.m.
Description:	All day big brunch £2.99 includes 2 sausages, 2 bacon rashers, 2 eggs, beans, tomato, hash brown, toast and butter.
Petrol:	Available 24 hours on site.
Comments:	My principal memory of this store is that it was the beginning of a drive from Carlisle to Berwick-upon-Tweed through the Scottish lowlands, idyllic country. It was a beautiful spring morning and the sound of the rivers and birds singing made me feel good to be alive.

Meggan Curry
College Farm
Preston St Mary
Suffolk.
3/4/2000.
via St Mawes
Cornwall

Dear Vincent,

Your bode is a "God send", + thank you so much, for writing this little masterpiece. The bode is simplicity itself to use, + saved us pounds on petrol + food. All "us" weary travellers of motorways need, are inexpensive good food, fuel at competitive prices + clean loos, not these outer space machines that swallow your money, expensive food, (where do they get it from?! Russia?!?) + fuel at inflated prices. They are "carbuncles" of poor quality on our motorways, leaving the poor Mowrist "poorer" + more frustrated on leaving them.

Once again, many thanks for this brilliant bode, which now has a permanent position beside the map bode in the car.

Yours sincerely
Meggan.

Tesco *M11/Junction 8*
Bishops Park Centre
Bishop's Stortford

Tel: 01279 697600

Location: At junction 8 take the A120 west which runs over the top of Bishop's Stortford. The store is on the fourth roundabout and lies 4 miles from the junction.

Hours:

Monday - Friday	8.00 a.m. - 8.00 p.m.
Saturday	7.30 a.m. - 8.00 p.m.
Sunday	10.00 a.m. - 4.00 p.m.

Description: The all day brunch is £2.99 and includes 2 sausages, 2 bacon rashers, 2 eggs, beans, tomato, hash brown, toast and butter.

Petrol:

On site Monday - Saturday	7.00 a.m. - 10.30 p.m.
Sunday	8.00 a.m. - 8.00 p.m.

Comments: Superbly positioned for Stansted bound holiday traffic as well as M11 traffic bound for the north.

It was here that on the 11th March 1999 that this store was compared with the Welcome Break at Birchanger Green at junction 8 of the M11. The Tesco all day brunch was 55% the price of the Red Hen Special breakfast at £5.45 and Tesco's unleaded petrol was 7 pence per litre cheaper. Further comment is unnecessary.

Tesco *A604*
Abbots Ripton Road
Huntingdon

Tel: 01480 327400

Location: The A604 becomes the A14 at Huntingdon. At that point take the A141 to Huntingdon and at the roundabout after 0.5 mile take the second exit marked Stukeley Meadows Industrial Area. Tesco is on the right after 1 mile therefore 1.5 miles from the point where the A604/A14 meet.

Hours:

Monday	8.00 a.m. - 8.00 p.m.
Tuesday - Saturday	7.00 a.m. - 8.00 p.m.
Sunday	10.00 a.m. - 4.00 p.m.

Description: New Magnificent 7 £1.99 until noon.
The all day brunch is £2.99

Petrol: On site 24 hours, 7 days.

Comments: The store is used occasionally by John and Norma Major who apparently have a penchant for the pizzas here. Well located for traffic moving between the A1/M11 motorways.

Sainsbury's ***M20/Junction 5***
Mills Road
Quarry Wood
Maidstone

Tel: 01622 790223

Location:	At junction 5 take the A20 Maidstone Road. At the roundabout turn right towards West Malling and Sainsbury's is on the left 0.8 mile from junction 5.

Hours:

Monday and Tuesday	8.00 a.m. - 6.30 p.m.
Wednesday	8.00 a.m. - 7.00 p.m.
Thursday and Friday	8.00 a.m. - 8.00 p.m.
Saturday	8.00 a.m. - 7.00 p.m.
Sunday	9.30 a.m. - 3.30 p.m.

Description: Breakfast at £1.95 plus the brunch all day at £3.10.

Petrol:

On site, Monday - Saturday	6.00 a.m. - 10.15 p.m.
Sunday	7.00 a.m. - 6.00 p.m.

Comments: By the time this book emerges there will be a new restaurant within the supermarket as a refurbishment programme was being carried out at the time of my inspection. Saleem in customer services proudly described the "5 after 5" whereby there are 5 set meals after 5.00 p.m. all less than £4.00. Buy one such meal and you get another free. The menu varies but usually includes fish and chips, vegetable lasagne and chilli and rice.

Sainsbury's *Simone Weil Avenue* *Ashford*

M20/Junction 9

Tel: 01233 610841

Location: The store actually backs onto the motorway. Take the A20 south to Ashford, turn left at the roundabout and the store is on the left 0.7 mile from junction 9.

Hours:

Monday - Thursday	8.00 a.m. - 7.00 p.m.
Friday and Saturday	8.00 a.m. - 6.30 p.m.
Sunday	9.30 a.m. - 3.00 p.m.

Description: Single breakfast £1.95, double breakfast £3.60 and the brunch is £3.10.

Petrol: On site 24 hours, 7 days.

Comments: Very convenient for traffic going out to (or returning from) the channel tunnel or Folkestone and Dover for ferry crossings. The staff told me that Vic Reeves was a visitor to the restaurant and seemed surprised when I said I'd never heard of him. They also said actress Jan Francis of "Just Good Friends" fame visited the store and were pleased when I said I was a fan of hers! I believe this store could open longer hours to cater for channel tunnel traffic either going or returning.

Tesco | *M20/Junction 12*

Cheriton High Street
Folkestone

Tel: 01303 719400

Location:	At junction 12 take the A20 into Folkestone. The store is on the right 0.1 mile from the junction.	
Hours:	Monday - Saturday Sunday	8.30 a.m. - 8.00 p.m. 10.00 a.m. - 4.00 p.m.
Description:	All day big brunch £2.99.	
Petrol:	On site 24 hours, 7 days.	
Comments:	The store is, at the time of writing, currently being refitted and the opening times will apply on completion of the work. Kay the restaurant manageress, told me that when delays take place on the Channel Tunnel passengers are actually sent over to Tesco close by for a meal and browse.	

Savacentre Barnet Road London Colney — *M25/Junction 22*

Tel: 01727 825000

Location:	North of junction 22 take the sign for London Colney. The store is 0.5 mile from junction 22 and lies adjacent to the motorway.	
Hours:	Monday - Wednesday	8.00 a.m. - 8.00 p.m.
	Thursday and Friday	8.00 a.m. - 9.00 p.m.
	Saturday	8.00 a.m. - 8.00 p.m.
	Sunday	10.00 a.m. - 4.00 p.m.
Description:	All day brunch £2.35 comprises 2 sausages, bacon, fried egg, fried bread, beans or any 6 breakfast items for £2.95.	
Petrol:	On site Monday - Saturday	5.30 a.m. - 10.30 p.m.
	Sunday	8.00 a.m. - 5.00 p.m.
Comments:	Several businessmen were having a breakfast meeting at the time of my inspection obviously preferring the prices here to those at the South Mimms services at the next junction on the M25.	

Truckstop *M25/Junction 23*
South Mimms

Tel: 01707 649998

Location: Immediately adjacent to junction 23 and located in the north east quadrant of the M25/A1 intersection.

Hours: Open continuously 24 hours per day apart from the period 2.00 p.m. on Saturday until 10.00 a.m. Sunday.

Description: The all day breakfast at £4.50 comprises 2 sausages, 2 bacon rashers, 2 fried eggs, beans, 3 hash browns, fried bread, toast, tea or coffee and includes a refill on the tea or coffee.

The traditional breakfast at the Welcome Break immediately adjacent costs £6.25 and only has 1 egg. Enough said.

Petrol: Not available on site so fill up elsewhere rather than paying the extortionate prices at the service station, 66.9 pence per litre for unleaded petrol on the day I called. Compare that to the Savacentre petrol price at London Colney at the next junction.

Comments: When comparing like with like, this one emerges immeasurably better than the service station adjacent.

P
SERVICE
AREA
PARKING

Tesco *M25/Junction 24*
Mutton Lane
Potters Bar

Tel: 01707 347500

Location: The store is 0.6 mile north of junction 24 through the traffic lights and on the right hand side.

Hours:

Monday - Saturday	8.00 a.m. - 8.00 p.m.
Sunday	10.00 a.m. - 4.00 p.m.

Description: The big brunch once again rescued me on a cold February morning, price £2.99.

Petrol: There are plans to install a petrol station on site but at the time of my inspection petrol is available 24 hours a day by going back down to the M25 and turning left at the traffic lights. The petrol station is a few yards down on the left.

Comments: Bill served me breakfast and when he heard the reason for my visit expressed a great interest in the book. By the way, I had scrambled eggs this time instead of a fried egg.

Tesco *Lakeside* *Thurrock* — *M25/Junction 31*

Tel: 01708 791400

Location: Access is easier from junction 31 rather than junction 30. Come off at junction 31 and take the A1306. At the roundabout take the signs to "Retail Park" and at the next roundabout turn down the side of McDonald's to Tesco which is less than 1 mile from the junction.

Hours:

Monday	8.00 a.m. - 8.00 p.m.
Tuesday - Saturday	7.00 a.m. - 8.00 p.m.
Sunday	10.00 a.m. - 4.00 p.m.

Description: All day brunch £2.99.

Petrol: On site 24 hours, 7 days.

Comments: Part of a massive retail park, has a nice conservatory forming part of the restaurant.

Tesco **_M27/Junction 8_**

Hamble Lane
Bursledon Towers
Southampton

Tel: 01703 297500

Location:	Turn left at the roundabout immediately adjacent to junction 8. At the next small roundabout the Tesco store is clearly visible and sign posted and lies 0.5 mile from junction 8.	
Hours:	Monday Tuesday - Saturday Sunday	8.00 a.m. - 10.00 p.m. 7.00 a.m. - 10.00 p.m. 10.00 a.m. - 4.00 p.m.
Description:	The ubiquitous all day brunch at £2.99 goes down well.	
Petrol:	On site 24 hours, 7 days.	
Comments:	Immensely popular, following a refurbishment, with office executives who have breakfast meetings here and holiday traffic heading for the Channel ports. Teresa Ortega in the restaurant was proud to emphasise its appeal to motorway traffic.	

Tesco *M27/Junction 12*

Clement Atlee Way
Portsmouth North Harbour
Portsmouth

Tel: 01705 307800

Location:	Take the slip road off junction 12 to the roundabout, turn left on Southampton Road and the Tesco is on the left 0.2 mile from the junction and clearly visible from the slip road.	
Hours:	Monday - Saturday Sunday	8.00 a.m. - 8.00 p.m. 10.00 a.m. - 4.00 p.m.
Description:	The all day brunch is £2.99 and includes 2 sausages, 2 bacon rashers, 2 eggs, beans, tomato, hash brown, toast and butter.	
Petrol:	On site 24 hours, 7 days.	
Comments:	Immensely popular with Europe bound ferry traffic who wish to fill up with food and petrol prior to indulging in Euro currency.	

Tesco *M32/Junction 2*
Eastgate Road
Bristol

Tel: 0117 912 7400

Location:	The property is immediately to the west of junction 2 and is clearly visible from the motorway.	
Hours:	Monday Tuesday - Saturday Sunday	8.00 a.m. - 8.00 p.m. 7.00 a.m. - 8.00 p.m. 10.00 a.m. - 4.00 p.m.
Description:	All day big brunch at £2.99 comprises 2 sausages, 2 bacon rashers, 2 fried eggs, beans, tomato, chips or hash brown and bread and butter.	
Petrol:	On site 24 hours, 7 days.	
Comments:	Eminently suitable for either M4 or M5 West Country bound traffic as the detour is minimal. Easily recognisable too with a roof design somewhat reminiscent of that caricature of opulence, the Millennium Dome.	

Asda *M40/Junction 4*
Holmers Farm Way
High Wycombe

Tel: 01494 441611

Location:	Immediately north of junction 4 take the first left on John Hall Way. Turn first left into Crest Road passing the U.C.I. Cinema on the left. The store is further down on the left hand side and lies 0.5 mile from junction 4.
Hours:	Monday - Saturday 7.30 a.m. - 8.30 p.m. Sunday 9.30 a.m. - 3.30 p.m.
Description:	The Asda big brunch at £2.79 including tea or coffee is excellent value and at 11.30 a.m. replaces the similarly priced Asda breakfast.
Petrol:	On site 24 hours apart from the period 11.00 p.m. on Sunday until 6.30 a.m. on Monday morning.
Comments:	A large modern store well tailored to M40 traffic with a hearty appetite. Clearly visible from the motorway.

Tesco *M40/Junction 11*
Lockheed Close
Banbury

Tel: 01295 457400

Location: At junction 11 take the A422 to Banbury. The store is adjacent to the third roundabout 1.1 miles from junction 11. Go straight across at the roundabout to get into the car park.

Hours:

Monday - Friday	8.00 a.m. - 8.00 p.m.
Saturday	7.30 a.m. - 8.00 p.m.
Sunday	10.00 a.m. - 4.00 p.m.

Description: The Magnificent 7 breakfast at £1.99 comprises bacon, sausage, fried egg, beans, tomato, hash browns, toast and butter.

The all day big brunch is £2.99.

Petrol: On site 24 hours, 7 days.

Comments: Excellent stopping point midway twixt London and Birmingham.

Tesco ***M42/Junction 4***
Stratford Road
Solihull

Tel: 0121 253 7500

Location: At junction 4 take the A34 into Solihull. The store is on the left at the roundabout 0.2 mile from the junction.

Hours:

Monday	8.00 a.m. - 8.00 p.m.
Tuesday - Saturday	7.00 a.m. - 8.00 p.m.
Sunday	9.30 a.m. - 4.00 p.m.

Description: The all day big brunch at £2.99 comprises 2 eggs, 2 bacon rashers, 2 sausages, hash browns, beans, tomato, bread and butter.
In the afternoon chips substitute for the hash browns.

Petrol: On site 24 hours, 7 days.

Comments: I was informed that the store has been visited by both Jasper Carrott and Karren Brady. "Karren who?" said I. Two days later she was on television. To the uninitiated she is the M.D. of Birmingham City F.C. The store serves the Birmingham end of the M40 and is an excellent stopping off point for West Country traffic from the north.

NEW MAGNIFICENT 7
1·99

26.3.00.

Gable End,
5 Lilac Close,
Addingham.
W. Yorks LS29 0SF.

Dear Vincent

Many thanks for sending the copy of Duffy's Cheaper Choices.

Motorway journeys, with this book in the glove compartment, will at long last hold some enjoyable stops. The book fills a gap which no Service Station (?) can match.

You should be nominated for the Honours List for your services to motorists.

With every best wish for your future publications, and thanks to you, your wife & family, - not forgetting the typist!

Sincerely
Margaret Campbell

Sainsbury's *M53/Junction 10*
Ellesmere Port
Cheshire

Tel: 0151 357 3181

Location:	The store is immediately adjacent to junction 10 on the west side of the motorway. Access to and from Manchester is via junction 15 M56.	
Hours:	Monday - Wednesday	8.30 a.m. - 7.00 p.m.
	Thursday - Friday	8.30 a.m. - 8.00 p.m.
	Saturday	8.00 a.m. - 6.00 p.m.
	Sunday	10.00 a.m. - 4.30 p.m.
Description:	Sainsbury's brunch £3.10. Also there is a lighter breakfast at £1.95 comprising 2 sausages, 2 bacon rashers, fried egg and beans.	
Petrol:	Available on site	
	Monday - Friday	6.00 a.m. - 10.00 p.m.
	Saturday	6.00 a.m. - 9.00 p.m.
	Sunday	8.00 a.m. - 6.00 p.m.

Comments:

I particularly remember this store as I drove straight through junction 10 as the music from Tchaikovsky's "Sleeping Beauty" completely took my attention. Adjacent to the store, there is a McArthur Glen Shopping Centre where a family could quite happily spend a few hours. This too has a lavish foodcourt.

N.B. There is no access to westbound traffic on the M56 from the M53 so at junction 10 M53, take the A5117 to junction 16 M56. Treat similarly if visiting the store coming from Wales.

Truckstop *M54/Junction 1*
Cannock Road
Wolverhampton

Tel: 01902 307535

Location: Immediately to the south of junction 1 around 0.2 mile from that junction and adjacent to the A460. The facility is also easily accessible from junction 11 M6.

Hours: Open continuously 24 hours per day apart from the period commencing 2.00 p.m. Saturday until 10.00 a.m. Sunday.

Description: All day breakfast 2 sausages, 2 eggs, 2 bacon rashers, beans, 3 hash browns, fried bread £4.50.

Petrol: On site 24 hours per day.

Comments: I was given a guided tour by a certain John Duffy (no relation), a maintenance supervisor who proudly demonstrated the shop, showers, television room and log cabin style restaurant. The hygiene would have been a tribute to an operating theatre.

Sainsbury's Colliers Way Telford — *M54/Junction 5*

Tel: 01952 299702

Location: Take the road due south of junction 5 to Telford and go straight across at the first roundabout into Hall Park Way. Turn right at the next roundabout to Sainsbury's which is 0.4 mile from junction 5.

Hours:

Monday - Friday	8.00 a.m. - 8.00 p.m.
Saturday	8.00 a.m. - 7.00 p.m.
Sunday	9.30 a.m. - 3.30 p.m.

Description: Breakfast till 11.30 a.m. becomes the all day brunch thereafter. 2 sausages, 2 bacon rashers, egg, beans or tomatoes, chips £3.10. There is also a breakfast at £1.95 comprising bacon, sausage, egg, hash brown, beans or tomatoes and toast and twice the amount at £3.60.

Petrol: On site 7 days 6.00 a.m. - midnight.

Comments: An excellent stop off for Wales bound traffic from the West Midlands motorway network, M6, M5 etc.

Tesco *M55/Junction 4*
Clifton Road
Blackpool

Tel: 01253 617500

Location:	Westbound traffic turn right at junction 4 on the A583 and first left into Clifton Road. Tesco is on the left hand side 0.85 mile from junction 4 and is visible from the motorway.	
Hours:	Monday	8.30 a.m. - 8.00 p.m.
	Tuesday - Saturday	7.30 a.m. - 8.00 p.m.
	Sunday	9.30 a.m. - 4.00 p.m.
Description:	All day big brunch £2.99.	
Petrol:	On site 24 hours, 7 days.	
Comments:	Very popular at weekends and particularly during the summer months with the influx of holidaymakers. There are also car boot sales on adjacent land periodically.	

Asda *M60/Junction 10*
Barton Dock Road
Trafford
Manchester

Tel: 0161 748 5841

Location: From junction 10 take the sign towards the Trafford Shopping Centre. Turn first right onto Barton Dock Road and Asda is on the left 0.8 mile from junction 10.

Hours: Open 24 hours from 8.00 a.m. Monday until 8.00 p.m. Saturday.
Sunday 10.00 a.m. - 3.00 p.m.

Description: All day set breakfast at £2.79 comprises 2 sausages, 2 bacon rashers, egg, 2 hash browns, beans, tomato, mushrooms, plus any hot drink and is replaced at 11.30 a.m. by the similarly priced brunch.

Petrol: On site, available 24 hours from 8.00 a.m. Monday until 10.00 p.m. Saturday.
Sunday 9.00 a.m. - 6.00 p.m.

Comments: Very large new building directly opposite the Trafford Shopping Centre.

Tesco ***M60/Junction 17***
Bury New Road
Prestwich
Manchester

Tel: 0161 910 9400

Location:	Fronts A56 0.1 mile south of junction 17 towards Manchester. This used to be junction 17 M62.
Hours:	Open 24 hours from 7.00 a.m. Monday through till 8.00 p.m. Saturday. Sunday 10.00 a.m. - 4.00 p.m.
Description:	All day big brunch £2.99 comprises 2 sausages, 2 bacon rashers, 2 fried eggs, beans, tomato, hash brown, toast and butter.
Petrol:	Available 24 hours on site.
Comments:	Superb value for money and could not be closer to the motorway. Claire who served me, lives at nearby Radcliffe and asked if I could mention her in my book. Good on you Claire!

Asda
Middlebrook
Horwich

M61/Junction 6

Tel: 01204 699337

Location: Take A6027 east of junction 6, turn left at Bolton Wanderers new Reebok Stadium; Asda is on the right hand side 1.0 mile from junction 6.

Hours:

Monday - Wednesday	8.00 a.m. - 10.00 p.m.
Thursday, Friday	8.00 a.m. - Midnight
Saturday	8.00 a.m. - 10.00 p.m.
Sunday	11.00 a.m. - 5.00 p.m.

Description: The set breakfast at £2.79 includes 2 sausages, 2 bacon rashers, egg, 2 hash browns, beans, tomato, mushrooms plus any hot drink and is replaced by the brunch at 11.30 a.m.

Petrol: On site

Monday - Wednesday and Saturday	7.30 a.m. - 10.30 p.m.
Thursday, Friday	7.30 a.m. - Midnight
Sunday	9.00 a.m. - 6.00 p.m.

Comments: Actually forms part of a large retail park, ideal if you wish to spend all day shopping. Exceptional if all you want is the breakfast, fill up on petrol and move on.

Tesco **M62/Junction 20**
Silk Street
Rochdale

Tel: 01706 706600

Location:	From junction 20 take the A627 (M) towards Rochdale. At the roundabout turn left onto Edinburgh Way. Tesco is at the bottom of this road on the left hand side and is 1.5 miles from junction 20.	
Hours:	Monday Tuesday - Saturday Sunday	8.00 a.m. - 8.00 p.m. 7.00 a.m. - 8.00 p.m. 10.00 a.m. - 4.00 p.m.
Description:	All day big brunch £2.99	
Petrol:	Available on site 24 hours a day, 7 days a week.	
Comments:	An extended and refurbished store. I remember a hearty breakfast here at 7.00 a.m. on a cold wintry February morning prior to my assault on the Manchester conurbation. The staff were at pains to point out the extensive vegetarian menu.	

The Horncastle *M62/Junction 26*
Cleckheaton

Tel: 01274 875444

Location:	At junction 26 take the A638 sign posted Cleckheaton and Dewsbury. The pub is after 0.5 mile on the right hand side, parking is at the rear.
Landlord:	Bob Westcott.
Hours:	7 days 7.30 a.m. - 2.00 p.m.
Description:	Breakfast comprises bacon, fried egg, sausage, beans, mushrooms, black pudding, fried bread, toast and tea or coffee, all for £1.95.
Petrol:	Available at Tesco in nearby Cleckheaton. Monday - Saturday 6.30 a.m. - 8.30 p.m. Sunday 8.30 a.m. - 4.30 p.m. Turn right out of The Horncastle and after 0.5 mile take a right into Horncastle Street. Go to the top and the petrol station is in Tesco's car park.
Comments:	Excellent value for money and a good alternative to the Hartshead services close by.

Morrisons Stuart Road Pontefract — *M62/Junction 32*

Tel: 01977 600808

Location: At junction 32 take the A639 to Pontefract, the racecourse will be on the right. Go past the retail park and immediately after the sign for Pontefract and Tanshelf Railway Station, turn left, there is a sign saying "Tanshelf Industrial Estate". Morrisons is on the right further down some 1.4 miles from the junction.

Hours:

Monday - Saturday	8.00 a.m. - 6.30 p.m.
Sunday	10.00 a.m. - 3.00 p.m.

Description: Morrisons famous big breakfast £2.89 comprises 2 hash browns, 2 bacon rashers, sausage, fried bread, fried egg, beans, mushrooms and tomato.

Petrol: None on site. Use the services at A1/M62 crossroads if you must but you will be paying their prices. There is a petrol station 100 yards north of the junction fronting the A639 open 6.00 a.m. till 11.00 p.m. every day.

Comments: A large, airy spacious restaurant frequented, I was told, by Gary Rhodes of "Ready Steady Cook" fame and Graham Steadman, the Castleford R.L.F.C. coach.

Morrisons *M606*
Mayo Avenue
Bradford

Tel: 01274 727676

Location: At the Bradford end of the M606 go straight across at the roundabout on the Ring Road A6177. Morrisons is further down on the left hand side some 0.35 mile from the end of the M606.

Hours:

Monday - Wednesday	8.30 a.m. - 7.00 p.m.
Thursday and Friday	8.30 a.m. - 9.45 p.m.
Saturday	8.00 a.m. - 7.00 p.m.
Sunday	10.00 a.m. - 3.00 p.m.

Description: Morrisons famous big breakfast, 3 bacon rashers, sausage, fried egg, mushrooms, beans, hash browns, tomato, fried bread £2.89.

Petrol: On site, Sajeed reliably informed me that the hours were

Monday - Saturday	7.00 a.m. - 10.00 p.m.
Sunday	8.00 a.m. - 8.00 p.m.

Comments: Superb value for money although I did feel that the store and restaurant could open at least 30 minutes earlier to catch the substantial number who want an early breakfast. They do a fish and chip special every night at only £1.99.

Morrisons ***M621/Junction 5***
Church Street
Hunslet
Leeds

Tel: 0113 270 4711

Location: Going into Leeds leave junction 5 and turn right to Hunslet. Hunslet Parish church (opposite Morrisons) is clearly visible. At the roundabout take the second exit down the side of Tulip Retail Park. Morrisons is at the traffic lights further down 0.4 mile from junction 5. Take care to turn left at the lights so as to get in the car park.

Hours:

Monday - Wednesday	7.00 a.m. - 8.30 p.m.
Thursday and Friday	7.00 a.m. - 10.00 p.m.
Saturday	7.00 a.m. - 8.30 p.m.
Sunday	8.00 a.m. - 7.30 p.m.

Description: Morrisons famous big breakfast, 3 bacon rashers, sausage, fried egg, mushrooms, beans, hash browns, fried bread and tomato, £2.89.

Petrol:

On site Monday - Wednesday	7.00 a.m. - 8.30 p.m.
Thursday and Friday	7.00 a.m.- 10.00 p.m.
Saturday	7.00 a.m. - 8.30 p.m.
Sunday	8.00 a.m. - 7.00 p.m.

Comments: Spoke to Nigel Porter who was having breakfast at an adjacent table. He had driven up from London for a business meeting and expressed great interest in my book saying that he always used the supermarkets for a quick bite on his travels, where he could find one. Curiously, the Graham Wilson memorial rugby league trophy awarded to outstanding local youngsters was on display. A certain Jason Robinson won it in 1990-91.

Hi Peter

You mentioned the other day your friend
who is/has produced a book re alternative
eating for Motorway travellers.
Is his surname Duffy - a Chartered Surveyor?
If so I heard a Radio 5 Live interview with him
on 'Drive Time' with Peter Allen. (apprx 1645hrs)
Very favourable and program rcvd lots of e-mails from listeners
requesting repeat of book title.
Looks like a best seller!
I will be buying a copy needless to say. (I absolutely hate Granada
Svc areas - further north you go the more disgusting they are!).

Regards
John

I'M HUNGRY
I NEED THE TOILET
NEED A BREAK?
YUM YUM
MMMMM
BIG BREAKFAST 2·79

Sainsbury's Hitchin Road Stevenage — *A1/Junction 8*

Tel: 01438 759602

Location: Take the A602 east of junction 8 and the store is on the right hand side 0.2 mile from the junction.

Hours:

Monday - Wednesday	8.00 a.m. - 7.00 p.m.
Thursday	8.00 a.m. - 8.00 p.m.
Friday	8.00 a.m. - 9.00 p.m.
Saturday	7.30 a.m. - 7.00 p.m.
Sunday	9.30 a.m. - 4.00 p.m.

Description: Single breakfast £1.95. Double breakfast £3.60. The breakfast finishes at 11.30 a.m. and the brunch takes over therefrom both at £3.10 and includes 2 sausages, 2 bacon rashers, egg, chips, beans or tomato.

Petrol:

On site Monday - Saturday	6.00 a.m. - 10.30 p.m.
Sunday	7.30 a.m. - 8.00 p.m.

Comments: Unleaded petrol here was 62.9 pence per litre on the day I called. On the same day the service station at Toddington (M1 adjacent) was charging 66.9 pence for the same petrol. Further comment is unnecessary. Note the "5 after 5" described at the Maidstone outlet.

Tesco **_A1/Junction 17_**
Serpentine Green
Hampton
Peterborough

Tel: 01733 410500

Location:	At junction 17 take the A1139 to Peterborough. Turn right at the third roundabout and the store is on the right hand side 2.5 miles from junction 17.	
Hours:	Monday - Friday	8.00 a.m. - 8.00 p.m.
	Saturday	7.00 a.m. - 8.00 p.m.
	Sunday	9.30 a.m. - 4.00 p.m.

Description: All day big brunch £2.99 comprises 2 sausages, 2 eggs, 2 bacon rashers, beans, tomato, 2 hash browns.

Petrol: On site 24 hours, 7 days.

Comments: This is the largest purpose built Tesco in the U.K. at 130,000 sq.ft. and had only been open 2 weeks when I called with my children. Louise suggested "Duffy's Motorway Quest" as an appropriate title and my younger daughter Julie's contribution was "Duffy's Tests for the Best". A bit further from the junction than usual but access is simplicity itself and the breakfast was excellent!

Morrisons
Wetherby Road
Boroughbridge

A1/Junction 48

Tel: 01423 323211

Location: At junction 48 go to the roundabout on the east side of the A1 and take the road marked "Services/ Boroughbridge". The "services" actually refers to Morrisons which is further down on the left 0.5 mile from junction 48.

Hours:

Monday - Thursday	8.30 a.m. - 7.00 p.m.
Friday	8.30 a.m. - 8.00 p.m.
Saturday	8.00 a.m. - 7.00 p.m.
Sunday	10.00 a.m. - 4.00 p.m.

Description: Morrisons famous big breakfast, £2.89.

Petrol:

On site Monday - Thursday	8.30 a.m. - 8.00 p.m.
Friday	8.00 a.m. - 9.00 p.m.
Saturday	8.00 a.m. - 8.00 p.m.
Sunday	10.00 a.m. - 4.00 p.m.

Comments: This store gets a lot of coach and holiday traffic in summer. The restaurant is to be extended although Yvonne who attended to my needs believed that they could vastly increase their custom by opening 30 minutes earlier even if that meant the restaurant closed 30 minutes earlier.

Safeway *A1*
Eleventh Avenue
Team Valley
Gateshead

Tel: 0191 491 1627

Location: Lies immediately adjacent to the A1 at Gateshead at the junction marked "Team Valley Retail World" on the east side of the motorway and clearly visible.

Hours:

Monday - Wednesday	8.00 a.m. - 8.00 p.m.
Thursday and Friday	8.00 a.m. - 9.00 p.m.
Saturday	8.00 a.m. - 8.00 p.m.
Sunday	10.00 a.m. - 5.00 p.m.

Description: The big brunch at £3.09 is a hearty meal for the famished motorist and very reasonably priced.

Petrol:

On site Monday - Wednesday	7.00 a.m. - 10.00 p.m.
Thursday and Friday	7.00 a.m. - 10.30 p.m.
Saturday	7.00 a.m. - 10.00 p.m.
Sunday	8.00 a.m. - 8.00 p.m.

Comments: The junction immediately to the south of this store, i.e. the A1/A167, hosts the "Angel of the North" sculpture by Antony Gormley described by the critics as "eerily magnificent" but it's also an excellent landmark for the Safeway store half a mile to the north.

Safeway *A1*
North Road
Berwick-upon-Tweed

Tel: 01289 302200

Location:	Lies 1 mile north of Berwick town centre immediately adjacent to the A1 at its junction with the A1167.

Hours:

Monday - Friday	8.30 a.m. - 9.00 p.m.
Saturday	8.00 a.m. - 8.00 p.m.
Sunday	10.00 a.m. - 4.00 p.m.

Description: Apart from the all day breakfast at £1.99, the big brunch is £3.09 available after 11.30 a.m. and comprises 2 sausages, 2 eggs, 2 bacon rashers, tomatoes or beans, chips, bread and butter.

Petrol:

Monday - Saturday	7.00 a.m. - 10.30 p.m.
Sunday	8.00 a.m. - 8.00 p.m.

Comments: Bracing sea views and my gratitude to Rob Foote, the customer service manager, for his hospitality and help. Peter Wilson, head of commercial property finance at Halifax plc, suggested this one after he bought the first edition of my book. Cheers Peter!

To compare like with like (and also to prove my point) this big brunch is 44% of the price of the Full Monty breakfast on offer at Granada's Service Stations on the motorway.

By the way, Rob told me that Monica Lewinsky had used the petrol station.

Safeway *A2*
Coldharbour Road
Gravesend

Tel: 01474 331409

Location: Immediately adjacent to the A2, on the north side of this road at the crossroads with the A227 and 1.5 miles south of Gravesend. The M2, which is a continuation of the A2, commences 4 miles to the east.

Hours:

Monday - Wednesday	8.00 a.m. - 7.30 p.m.
Thursday - Saturday	8.00 a.m. - 8.30 p.m.
Sunday	10.00 a.m. - 3.00 p.m.

Description: The breakfast at £1.99 is replaced after 11.30 a.m. by the brunch at £3.09 which includes 2 fried eggs, 2 sausages, 2 bacon rashers, chips, beans or tomato, bread and butter.

Petrol:

On site Monday - Saturday	7.00 a.m. - 1.00 p.m.
Sunday	8.00 a.m. - 8.00 p.m.

Comments: Easily accessible to both eastbound and westbound traffic. Ann, in the restaurant, explained that the breakfast was exceptionally popular with people going to funerals at Medway Crematorium from London. I didn't know what to say to that. The M2 again eventually becomes the A2 leading to Dover.

Asda *A494*
Aston Road
Queensferry

Tel: 01244 822335

Location: The supermarket lies immediately to the north of the A494 Queensferry by-pass at its junction with the A548. It is highly conspicuous from the by-pass. It is at this point that the A550 become the A494.

Hours:

Monday - Wednesday	8.30 a.m. - 8.00 p.m.
Thursday and Friday	8.30 a.m. - 9.00 p.m.
Saturday	8.30 a.m. - 7.00 p.m.
Sunday	10.00 a.m. - 3.30 p.m.

Description: The Asda big breakfast at 10 items including a hot drink is available until 11.30 a.m. and costs £2.79. Thereafter the big brunch takes over at the same price.

Petrol:

On site Monday - Friday	7.00 a.m. - 10.30 p.m.
Saturday	7.00 a.m. - 8.30 p.m.
Sunday	9.00 a.m. - 5.00 p.m.

Comments: An excellent stop off for holiday traffic aiming for North Wales and Snowdonia and a natural link twixt the A55 and M56. Paula, in the restaurant, was at pains to point out the vociferous majority who spurn the service stations in favour of an Asda breakfast.

I had been vaguely aware of this one "en passant" when Denise and I went with our friends, Dave Mitchell and his wife, Beverley, on a rugby weekend to watch Mirfield Free Grammar on tour in Wales.

However, my mother-in-law's wish to visit her grandmother's grave in Llanrwst led to a family overnight in Llandudno, which led to our driving past this Asda again which in turn led to an entry in the book. Serendipity strikes another blow.

Thoughts by a man from Granada

Paul Kelly, Director of Granada Road Services, made the following comments on radio on my book. See his comments under "PK" and my own responses under "Author", my responses were made for this book.

PK: "If we look specifically at the example in Duffy's Cheaper Choices I think it was, supermarkets are not using their restaurants as a source of profits they're using them to encourage more people to come and shop.

Author: Yes Paul that is the title and what does the motorist care as to the intention of the retailer if the breakfast is less than half the price of your Full Monty?

PK: "I don't quite know why that one was particularly picked out" (referring to my citing the Full Monty breakfast at £6.99).

Author: Paul, a glass of orange juice and a copy of the Daily Express do not excuse virtually £7 for a breakfast. There's a pub adjacent to junction 26 of the M62 that does a massively superior breakfast at 28% of that price. There's plenty more in my book.

PK: "We welcome competition where there's genuine competition, this isn't necessarily genuine competition."

Author: Why not?

PK: "Our food stands comparison with comparable offers elsewhere."

Author: You certainly do not compare well with my comparables so where are your comparables?

PK: "It's important for us that people have the choice and that they can have a wide choice."

Author: They have now that my book is out.

PK: "We are in the business of catering to the needs of the travelling public."

Author: Thank you Paul, over and out.

AFTERWORD

The exercise has been completed and I will attempt to draw certain conclusions. I hope I have achieved a reasonable distribution throughout the motorway system. If the inhabitants of the north-east feel aggrieved, I apologise and will make reparation in a future edition.

Having completed the task I feel even more vehemently against these service stations as I did at the outset. I don't wish to portray myself as a walking advertisement for Tesco, Sainsbury's, Asda, Morrisons and Safeway, but for value for money with regard to hot food and petrol, the score is massively in favour of these outlets when compared with the motorway service stations. I do not exclude the Truckstops and other selections from this statement.

Time and again during my travels in compiling this book, I have met many people ranging from families on holiday to businessmen travelling long distances and have been pleasantly amazed by the eagerness with which they greet the announcement of my intention to publish the book which is only equalled by their distaste for the prices charged at the service stations. It seems to me that there is a healthy market demand for both the idea and contents therein and I only hope I have proved equal to the task.

Perhaps this work is a statement against the monopoly concept. If the balance has been redressed albeit slightly I have at least made a point.

V.P. Duffy
June 1999

AFTERWORD TO THIS EDITION

I trust that this second edition fills to some extent the vacuum left in the north-east by the first edition of my book.

I still feel the same contempt for these motorway service stations which prompted the book in the first place. In fact the disgust has probably increased over the last year and it is obviously my great hope that the book sells enough copies to reduce the amount of people who feel they have to use these facilities. It would give me great satisfaction to demolish their perceived monopoly concept. Perhaps they would then rethink their approach to price structuring and service.

V.P. Duffy
April 2000.

My grateful thanks to Fiona Roscoe who was a final year Graphic Arts student when she designed the cover and is now with a multi media company in Covent Garden. Fiona also helped with the drawings as did the pupils of St. John Fisher High School in Dewsbury and Fartown High School in Huddersfield. Finally, thank you Heather Moore for bearing with me in putting the manuscript onto a disc for the printer.